To with warm wishes Michael Christmas 2021

THE PEGASUS BRIDGE SHOW

The dramatic story of the capture of
Pegasus and Horsa Bridges during the
opening minutes of D-Day, 1944

MICHAEL BAWTREE

Michael Bawtree

Like No Other Press
155 Main Street
Wolfville NS
B4P 1C2
Canada

www.likenootherpress.ca

THE PEGASUS BRIDGE SHOW

ISBN 978-0-9919385-2-0

First published in Great Britain in 2021
by Mereo Books, an imprint of Memoirs Publishing

Canadian edition 2021
Copyright ©2021 Michael Bawtree

This book is sold subject to the condition that it shall not by way of trade or otherwise be lent, resold, hired out or otherwise circulated without the publisher's prior consent in any form of binding or cover, other than that in which it is published and without a similar condition, including this condition being imposed on the subsequent purchaser.

Printed and Bound in Canada by
Atlantic Digital, Halifax NS

Library and Archives Canada Cataloguing in Publication
Bawtree, Michael
The Pegasus Bridge Show / Michael Bawtree.

The address and e-mail for Like No Other Press can be
found at www.likenootherpress.ca

ISBN 978-0-9919385-2-0
Typeset in 11/15 pt Century Schoolbook
by Wiltshire Associates

BY THE SAME AUTHOR

Play
The Last of the Tsars

Non-Fiction
The New Singing Theatre

For Young Adults
Joe Howe to the Rescue

Memoirs
As Far As I Remember
The Best Fooling

The stage version of The Pegasus Bridge Show was commissioned in 2008 by Project65 (now Veterans Charity) to celebrate the 65th Anniversary of the participation of men of the 52nd of Foot, the Royal Engineers and the Glider Pilot Regiment in the first Allied operation on D-Day, June 6th, 1944.

Acknowledgements

I owe thanks to many people who were involved in helping me put together this book version of The Pegasus Bridge Show. They include Penny Bates, daughter of John Howard, who encouraged me to get it into print; Roy Bailey, my old comrade from A Company, Oxfordshire and Buckinghamshire Light Infantry 1957-8, who assisted me with the location and selection of illustrations; Terry Aulenbach, who helped me prepare the images for publication; Danny Greeno of Veterans Charity for his support of the project; Chris Newton and his colleagues at Mereo Books for editing and design; and General Sir Robert Pascoe, who first proposed the idea of the show and produced its 2008 tour, and who graciously provided the introduction to this book.

M.B.
July 2021

Foreword

by General Sir Robert Pascoe, KCB, MBE

This book, the Pegasus Bridge story, is Michael Bawtree's latest telling of the capture of Pegasus Bridge following his successful performances of the "Pegasus Bridge Show" in 2008. I am delighted that he asked me to write these few introductory remarks. As an officer of the Oxfordshire and Buckinghamshire Light Infantry (43rd & 52nd), I have long been aware of the heroic action of Major John Howard's men who fought with such distinction in our 2nd Battalion during World War II.

There were in fact two bridges to be captured. As well as the now famous one over the Caen canal, the other bridge, a few hundred yards to the East, spanned the tidal River Orne. They are now widely known as Pegasus and Horsa Bridges. The story of the operation has been told many times over since that dramatic action took place in the first hour of D-Day on 6th June 1944.

The tale presented in the "Pegasus Bridge Show" however, was unique. Not only because it was conceived, written and presented by a former officer, Michael Bawtree, who had served in the Regiment that carried out the operation, and who drew on the memories of some of those involved, but also because it was a presentation with original words and music that set the event within the history of previous cross-Channel campaigns.

It's now over 13 years since the "Pegasus Bridge Show", a fund raiser for Project 65, was enjoyed by audiences in Bath, RMA Sandhurst, Oxford and London. The actor Richard Todd, who landed by parachute in 1944 close to the bridges shortly after their capture - and later played the role of John Howard in the film `The Longest Day` - attended the performance held in Oxford

Town Hall and met some of the Veterans who also took part in the operation.

Michael went on to present his work in a DVD recording, produced in response to popular demand, which was created in the studio of Canadian film-maker David Sheehan, who both shot and edited the production in collaboration with Michael. This raised further funds for Project 65.

Michael Bawtree was born in Australia, grew up in England and like me, was a fellow subaltern in 1956-57, serving in the Oxford and Bucks when the Battalion was stationed in the Limassol District of Cyprus during the EOKA campaign.

After his National Service in the Regiment Michael made his home in Canada, where he enjoyed a distinguished career as a stage director, writer, actor and educator. He was awarded the Queen's Jubilee Medal in 2002 for services to the community.

The "Pegasus Bridge Show" was first a live stage performance, then a DVD and now the story comes as a book version, giving yet more people the opportunity to learn of the 'men in gliders' through Michael`s dramatic telling of the tale.

Once again, he has generously allowed any profits from the sale of his work to go to the support of veterans. For this Canadian edition, as an active member of his local Royal Canadian Legion Branch in Wolfville, Nova Scotia, Michael has donated all net proceeds from sales in Canada to the Branch's '75 Fund', which is dedicated to the renovation of the century-old Wolfville Legion building. The renovations will make the building fully wheel-chair-accessible, and provide new spaces for resources and work-shops for veterans, to help them live happy and productive lives.

Robert Pascoe
Adjutant General 1988-91
The British Army

The author when a platoon commander in Cyprus, 1957

Over fifty years ago, as a young officer serving in Cyprus with the Oxfordshire and Buckinghamshire Light Infantry, I first heard the story of the Pegasus Bridge raid from three of the men who took part in it. One of them was my Company Commander, and though I was only a lowly National Service officer, he and his family became my friends for life. This is why I was happy many years later to be invited to re-create that fateful night for the stage, and to put it into the perspective of history. Because I have spent my life working in the theatre, I feel particularly proud to have revived the role of the epic poet of old, who picked up his lyre and sang of the exploits of the mighty heroes of Greece and Troy. Our story too is the stuff of myth.

The performance was later captured on video, and seen around the world on YouTube, raising more funds for Veterans Charity. Now, with their encouragement, the poem has found its way into print.

So: once upon a time . . .

CROSSING THE
CHANNEL, 1066-1944

We could trace this story far back, almost to the beginnings of our written history, when a Roman invasion force crossed the English Channel under Julius Caesar; or to the Dark Ages, when the Angles, the Saxons, the Danes, the Jutes and others sent their marauding ships across the narrow seas to plunder and burn and eventually to settle. But let us start in 1066, when yet another invading army, this time the Normans, established their beach-head at Hastings, killed King Harold, and founded a dynasty under William I: William the Conqueror.

But there was one major difference between those invasions and the one we commemorate tonight. All of them crossed from east to west or from south to north: from the mainland of Europe to the scattering of off-shore islands now called Britain and Eire. There were further attempts in the same direction, notably the Spanish with their Armada in 1588, and Napoleon's intense preparations for invasion before losing his fleet at the Battle of Trafalgar in 1805. And there were plenty of marauding raids, like the Dutch sweeping up the Medway and the Thames in 1667 and destroying many ships of the line. But after 1066 no hostile army ever again landed on British soil, unless, like the forces under the Duke of Monmouth in 1685 or under William of Orange in 1688, they came to press more or less legitimate claims to the throne of England. Even William the Conqueror gave this as his excuse for invasion.

Here, though, we celebrate an engagement which began with a crossing from west to east, from north to south: from the British Isles to the mainland of Europe. Did earlier invasion forces ever cross in the same direction? Of course they did. The Black Prince, Henry the Fifth, John Churchill, Duke of Marlborough, and Arthur Wellesley, Duke of Wellington, were just some of those who headed armies on to the mainland, where they won decisive battles.

Of all these campaigns, the one that has almost epic status for us is that of Henry the Fifth, when he lay siege to Harfleur and then led his sick and exhausted men to victory at Agincourt. The reason of course is that this adventure was chronicled on stage by William Shakespeare, who was busy in the 1590s celebrating the triumphs of Queen Elizabeth's family the Tudors, following the miraculous defeat (in battle but also by weather) of the Spanish

Armada. The English Channel features in the very first prologue:

> *"Suppose within the girdle of these walls*
> *Are now confined two mighty monarchies*
> *Whose high uprearèd and abutting fronts*
> *The perilous narrow ocean parts asunder."*

Successfully crossing the 'perilous narrow ocean', Henry in his speech to his men before Harfleur gives them the very model of all pep talks:

> *"Once more unto the breach, dear friends, once more,*
> *Or close the wall up with our English dead…*
> *I see you stand like greyhounds in the slips,*
> *Straining upon the start. The game's afoot:*
> *Follow your spirit; and upon this charge*
> *Cry 'God for Harry, England, and Saint George!"*

Like all war leaders from Agamemnon to Field Marshal Haig to George W. Bush, Henry trusts that God is on his side. But Shakespeare's play is far from being a glorification of war for its own sake. Walking around his camp, the night before the great battle, Henry comes upon ordinary soldiers discussing just this question:

"If the cause be not good," says Michael Williams, "the king himself hath a heavy reckoning to make. There be few die well that die in a battle."

Henry is tormented by the responsibility of risking his men's lives if the cause be not just.

> *"Upon the king! Let us our lives, our souls,*
> *Our debts, our careful wives,*
> *Our children and our sins lay on the king!*
> *We must bear all. O hard condition!"*

Henry's cause, just or not, was to regain possession of his French lands, won through past marriages. In fact as a result of his victories he was the only British king ever to be made also heir to the throne of France, though he died before he could claim both 'mighty monarchies'.

The Duke of Marlborough crossed the same perilous narrow ocean to oppose French interests in the War of Spanish Succession in the early 18th century, winning his greatest victory at Blenheim. The French Revolution threw up a different enemy in the person of Napoleon Bonaparte, and to oppose him Sir John Moore in 1808 led an army to Spain, where he died in the Retreat to Corunna:

> *"Not a drum was heard, not a funeral note,*
> *As his corse to the rampart we hurried…"*

Wellington replaced Moore and slowly rolled back the French armies of occupation from Portugal and Spain, then drove them north to Napoleon's abdication in Paris, and finally, after Napoleon's escape from Elba and brief re-assumption of control, to the Battle of Waterloo. Britain's continuing attempts to balance off the major European powers led to another fairly horrifying engagement in the Crimea, in the 1850s – the first war to be photographed. We wonder how much those armies knew what they were fighting for, and whether the cause was just. Certainly the Light Brigade did not know, when, as the result of a misunderstood order, they rode into the enemy's cannon and back again. In Tennyson's famous poem: "Theirs not to reason why, Theirs but to do and die." And they did.

CONVERSATION across the WATER

But with the expansion of Britain's trade empire, her armies were already sailing much further afield than the continent of Europe. Many battles were fought to gain or re-gain control of territories which had been wrested from their original inhabitants and then fought over by the competing colonial powers: above all France, Spain, Portugal and Holland. So my own adopted country, Canada, was won from the French by General Wolfe on the Heights of Abraham in 1759. And it was not long after this that Britain found itself fighting wars to try to hold on to her own colonial so-called 'possessions'. Of these the first and most significant was the lost War of American Independence, but in the late eighteenth century, and all through the nineteenth, the campaigns had moved to India, to Afghanistan, to China, to Africa. New territories were won, and battles won and lost.

And then, in the twentieth century, the competitive trade and territorial pressures of Europe exploded out of the Balkans in the First World War. British forces crossed the Channel in their millions to join France in a hideous trench war against Germany, while Russia and Italy matched themselves against Austro-Hungary and Turkey, with Australian, New Zealand and British troops attempting to outflank them in the disaster of Gallipoli. And by the end of this horrendous conflict – only ten years after the miraculous invention of flight – aerial combat, bombing and reconnaissance had been added to the lexicon of battle, and that perilous narrow ocean no longer guarded the fortress of England 'against infection and the hand of war.' But of course in the air, as on the sea, the narrow ocean could be crossed in both directions, as we shall see.

Why are we starting this commemoration with such a lengthy historical review? Because, running like a thin scarlet thread through the last two hundred and fifty years of this tapestry, is the story of a regiment: a family of soldiers who from generation to generation fought and died in its battles.

The regiment whose exploit we are focusing on is the 52nd of Foot. Is it possible to summarize a regiment's long history in just a few words? No, but they were first raised in 1775. In 1881 they became the 43rd and 52nd of foot, and in 1908 were named the Oxfordshire and Buckinghamshire Light Infantry, the title under which they served in both World Wars, and until 1958, when they became part of the Greenjackets Brigade. They became the first Battalion of the Royal Greenjackets in 1966, which in 2007 was absorbed into the newly formed Rifle Regiment as its fourth battalion.

Through these many campaigns all over the world, the 52nd did as they were bidden by their sometimes brilliant, sometimes confused generals and commanding officers, and by their often-confused governments of the day. The cause was sometimes a fine and necessary one, like the containment and final defeat of the monstrous genius Napoleon. But they were often fought to protect the shipping lanes of Britain's merchant navy, or to quell ancient inhabitants of conquered lands, or to suppress threats to the vast British Empire by beating out rival trading nations. Though modern hindsight might view these imperialist engagements as morally dubious, there was little doubt at the time that whatever the King or Queen demanded of a soldier must be, in the words of *1066 And All That*, 'a Good Thing'. And of course the Empire in its day was believed to be a Good Thing too.

The 52nd of Foot, along with their fellow Battalions of the 43rd, played a major role in Flanders and France in the First World War, crossing that perilous narrow ocean sometimes more than once until they fell, and exchanging the anxious but peaceful world of Great Britain for the living hell of Nonne Boschen, Ypres, Passchaendaele and the Menin Road, where so many perished:

> *"No mockery now for them, no prayers, no bells,*
> *Nor any voice of mourning save the choirs,*
> *The shrill, demented choirs of wailing shells,*
> *And bugles calling for them from sad shires."*

The regiment also served in Macedonia, and lost an entire battalion in Mesopotamia – now Iraq – against Germany's ally Turkey, the Ottoman Empire.

Following the 'war to end all wars', the 52nd, its battalion strength much reduced for 'peacetime', was sent briefly to Ireland and then to India, where it remained until 1940, reinforcing the Indian Army in their efforts to hold down the growing struggle for independence. But while they were fox-hunting and downing their *chota pegs* in Rawalpindi and other places, all was not well back in Europe.

The Treaty of Versailles of 1919 had unravelled. Germany's huge reparations requirements had beggared the country, increasingly split between a powerful communist party, supported by the newly minted Soviet Russia, and an extreme nationalist movement, led by one Adolf Hitler. England and France, exhausted by their efforts in the First World War, had allowed their military strength to decline: they could not face the prospect of more warfare, and were reluctant to enforce the punitive terms of the Versailles Treaty. When Hitler was narrowly elected Chancellor of Germany in 1933 there were even many British who saw him as a saviour of his country; and though he immediately embarked on his campaign to burn books, to suppress communists, Jews, gipsies and homosexuals, to rebuild the German army, navy and air force (in contravention of Versailles), and to gather and display his increasingly numerous zealots in fearsome events like the Nuremberg Rally, well at least he got Germany's economy functioning again, didn't he?

Even his monstrous eugenics program was seen by some as healthy, and was well supported by American funds. Winston Churchill's repeated warnings during the thirties fell largely on deaf ears. Winston was in the wilderness, with neither power nor credibility within his own party. He was seen as an unstable warmonger.

It was Hitler's policy of territorial expansion which finally forced England and France into action, and then only after allowing Austria to be overrun and Czechoslovakia to be thrown to the wolves the same year. Italy under Mussolini had now joined forces with Hitler in the Rome-Berlin Axis, and in August 1939, to the shock and horror of socialists all over the world, the Soviet Union signed a non-aggression pact with Hitler, including a secret agreement on how to carve up the Baltic States and Poland between them. In response to the Czech dismemberment, England and France had guaranteed the integrity of the Polish state. So when Hitler marched and flew into Poland on September 3rd, 1939, Britain and France had no alternative but to declare war on Germany and its allies. The Second World War had begun.

Was the cause good? There were many to blame for things coming to such a pass at the end of the thirties, but you will find very few who doubt that once Hitler was launched on his murderous plans for the Third Reich and the world, he could be stopped only by force of arms. Yes, of all wars ever fought, this was, and is, reckoned to be 'a just war', a war to save civilisation itself.

France mobilized, and before the end of the month Britain's Expeditionary Force had begun crossing the Channel to protect Belgium and France. The next few months were known as the Phoney War. Then in April, Hitler invaded Denmark and Norway. And on the 10th of May 1940, the German army struck, unleashing their western offensive through Belgium, Holland and Luxembourg and on into France. On the very same day, Winston Churchill became Prime Minister. His message for the House of Commons and for the country was a sombre one:

"We have before us an ordeal of the most grievous kind… But I take up my task with buoyancy and hope. I feel sure that our cause will not be suffered to fail among men… Let us go forward with our united strength."

Less than four weeks later in France, driven into a pocket against the sea, Britain had evacuated nearly a quarter of a million of its own soldiers – including a battalion of the 43rd – and over 100,000 French and Belgian troops, that spectacular defeat known as the miracle of Dunkirk. All heavy equipment was left behind. By the end of June the Wehrmacht had occupied Paris and the French had capitulated. Immediately Hitler launched preparations for Operation Sealion: the invasion of Britain. Churchill again.

"Upon this battle depends the survival of Christian civilisation. The whole fury and might of the enemy must very soon be turned on us. Hitler knows that he will have to break us in this island or lose the war."

A necessary prelude for the Nazi forces was to win supremacy in the skies. The Battle of Britain followed, in which a few hundred gallant Spitfire pilots held the Luftwaffe at bay and are credited with saving the country from invasion. In the immortal words of Churchill, "Never in the field of human conflict was so much owed by so many to so few." In September Hitler launched his devastating blitz against London, but he postponed his invasion and attacked Romania. The following year, in defiance of his non-aggression pact, he turned his forces against Soviet Russia, striking through Poland and Hungary.

The idea of a gallant 'few' who by their heroism have saved the many goes back into the distant history of warfare, from the three hundred Spartans who perished holding the pass at Thermopylae, to the single runner speeding from Marathon to Athens to bring news of the Greek land victory and the approaching Persian fleet, to Horatius holding the bridge and saving Rome, to Henry the Fifth's "*we few, we happy few, we band of brothers*". Because, even when vast numbers of troops are being manoeuvred across the landscape, or huge fleets sail the seas or mass in the skies, there are always those moments when a small group – even a single individual, or a ship, or a plane – happens to have a huge outcome depend on their actions at a critical moment at a critical place. The exploit we commemorate here is such a story.

You may wonder why we are beginning on such a vast canvas in time and space. But our story only makes sense in the context of the world events that swung around it. This is like one of those films in which the camera begins by revealing a vast panoramic landscape, and then slowly zooms in onto one tiny detail.

By August of 1940, in Churchill's own words, "the whole Western seaboard of Europe, from the North Cape to the Spanish frontier" was in German hands. Most of France, all Belgium, Holland, Denmark and Norway were overrun. Western Poland and Czechoslovakia were satellites. Greece, Romania, Hungary and Bulgaria were soon to be conquered. Britain stood alone. And even if it was "their finest hour", how on earth could one imagine that the tide could ever be reversed?

And yet from the very first, there was a determination that some day, somehow, that perilous narrow ocean would be crossed from west to east or north to south, and that Hitler's mighty divisions would be confronted and finally pushed back to Germany.

Churchill's instructions to his planners were clear: "You are to prepare for the invasion of Europe. You must devise and design the appliances, the landing craft, and the technique... The whole of the South Coast of England is a bastion of defence against the invasion of Hitler; you've got to turn it into the springboard for our attack."

The 52nd Light Infantry, returning from India in 1940, expected to be sent out to Belgium immediately, but the British Expeditionary Force was evacuated from Dunkirk a few weeks before they arrived in Liverpool. As a battalion at full strength and in fighting trim, they were a valuable resource, and in the next year and more were attached to an Independent Brigade and pushed around the country to fill gaps and prepare for Hitler's invasion. As the months went by they became more and more impatient to see action. But in October 1941, with the German invasion plans now apparently shelved, they were informed that the Brigade was to be converted to an 'airlanding brigade', within a newly formed 1st Airborne Division.

Airborne operations were a fairly recent development in European warfare. Companies of Hitler's paratroopers had been dropped and landed in gliders effectively in the invasions of Denmark and Norway, and then in Holland and Belgium. The next year both gliders and paratroopers were extensively employed in the invasion of Crete. It was a successful mission, but the Germans suffered very heavy losses, and apparently Hitler, not known to be squeamish, was horrified and forbade further airborne operations.

Meanwhile the British, who were not remarkable for forward thinking in the nineteen thirties, had developed no airlanding capacity of any sort before the war. They now, under Churchill's prodding, decided they must get into the game. And that is why at the end of 1941 we see the 52nd, now officially part of an airborne division, moving to a mushroom farm near Basingstoke to begin training. No one being entirely sure of their mission, they were simply ordered to achieve extraordinary individual fitness, with PT, road walks, runs, swimming lessons and forced marches. Then in April they joined the rest of the new Airborne Division in Bulford to begin air training. On their sleeves they wore flashes bearing the figure of the winged horse Pegasus, the badge which – legend has it – was proposed by the novelist Daphne du Maurier, whose husband was the dashing General 'Boy' Browning, first commander of the Airborne Division.

Meanwhile, huge events were unrolling across the Channel and further afield. Hitler's Operation Barbarossa bit deep into Soviet Russia. The Japanese overran the Far East, and then in December 1941 they struck the American fleet at Pearl Harbour, bringing the United States into the war. The British faced first Italy in North Africa, and then Rommel, with American forces joining Montgomery and the Eighth Army to fight and win their first engagements against Hitler.

The United States had wanted to attack across the Channel in 1942, soon after they joined the European War, but were persuaded by the British that it was too soon and that it would be a catastrophic disaster.

In 1942, and again 1943, Stalin was calling bitterly for a second front to be opened in the west to take the pressure off his grievously suffering armies and nation. It was still considered too soon for this, but preparations were finally in hand, and one of the weapons of the planned invasion was to be airborne. Other units of the 1st Airborne Division were mobilised in the glider and paratrooper attack on Sicily in April 1943. Those who successfully landed fought valiantly, but 75 gliders ditched into the sea. The 1st Airlanding Brigade lost 250 drowned and a further 50 missing, with 60 killed on land: the attacking parties were soon overwhelmed. Even now, there is real distress at what seems to have been insufficient planning and training for the operation, although weather was also to blame. If there was anything to be taken away from the disaster, it was to the advantage of the 52nd and the newly created 6th Airborne Division of which they were now a part. Many painful lessons were learned.

And now it is time to introduce some of the principal participants in the story of Pegasus and Horsa Bridges. Among the new men joining the regiment in early 1941 was one John Howard, recently a Regimental Sergeant Major and then a commissioned officer with the Kings Shropshire Light Infantry reserve battalion,

John Howard

then a bobby with the Oxford City Police, and now commissioned into the Oxford and Bucks, where as a Cockney boy promoted from the ranks he at first found himself out of place in the huntin', shootin' and fishin' officers' mess of the old county regiment. But his dedication was soon recognised and at the end of 1941 he was promoted first to captain and then to major, and given his own command: 'D' Company. His second-in-command was Brian Priday. His platoon commanders were Den Brotheridge, Tony Hooper, Harry Sweeney (of course nicknamed 'Tod') and the nineteen-year-old David Wood, fresh out of Officer Training.

He later had two other platoons transferred to his command from B Company. One of them was commanded by Sandy Smith, the other by Denis Fox.

And here I want to interject a personal note. When, as a National Service I came ashore at Limassol, Cyprus, in January 1957 from the good ship Asturias, to join the 1st Battalion Oxford and Bucks, I found myself attached to A company, commanded by one Tod Sweeney, by this time Major 'Tod' Sweeney MC. The Military Attaché to Field Marshal Lord Harding and then Sir Hugh Foot, Britain's Governors-General in Cyprus, was one Major Denis Fox MBE, who paid frequent visits to the Battalion. Soon to be second in command of our Battalion was one Major David Wood. And among our Company Serjeant Majors was Bill Bailey. All of these gentlemen took part in the event we commemorate in this book, and it was not long before Tod Sweeney, on some company exercise up in the hills of Cyprus, was persuaded by his young officers, one evening by the camp fire, to tell the story of the capture of Pegasus and Horsa Bridges. At that time his war exploits seemed to hail from the very distant past, and we both admired him for his 'old soldier' reminiscences, and also teased him. We were also taken well aback by learning that he had been a novice monk, leaving his monkish habit at the start of the war to enlist against the Führer, and later marrying his lovely wife Geraldine. He is in fact the only British soldier I have ever heard referred to as a saint.

From Tod we first learnt of the somewhat fearsome Major John Howard, and his part in the Pegasus Bridge operation, to which we now return.

Howard was determined from the beginning that his company, 'D' Company, was to be the best. In the words of David Wood:

"I quickly learned that Letter D Company had to be the best

at everything – shooting, football, boxing, cross-country running and above all marching. We marched for miles – my feet still feel sore when I go anywhere near Bulford. One standard test was 25 miles in 6 hours, in full battle order. John was really obsessed with fitness."

Howard's mania for fitness, of which of course he was his own supreme example, was described as "beyond anything the British Army had ever seen before." He was dealing with a company that was waiting to see some action, and was always aware that boredom and frustration were in the air as the months went by. One time the regiment was sent down to Devon for two months of rock climbing, and then ordered to march back the 130 miles to Bulford. Howard strode alongside his company, pushing them on. On the fourth day two of his soldiers, Bill Bailey and Wally Parr, came out on parade on their knees. Howard asked them what the blazes they were doing, and they replied they had worn away the bottom half of their legs. But they marched on. "Mad bastard," they muttered. But they marched. And D Company came in half a day ahead of

the rest of the regiment. From then on they were the shining lights of the battalion and could do nothing wrong. When a race was held to sort out the best runners in the whole Brigade, 'D' Company put in 20 runners, and they took fifteen of the first twenty places.

Since the regiment was being prepared for glider operations, gliders were naturally a major part of their training. They soon discovered the discomfort of being towed along behind a tug plane. General Crookenden described the sensation: "Since the glider on the end of its tug-rope moved in a series of surges as the tug-rope tightened and slackened, and was subject to the normal pitching, rolling and yawing of any aircraft, few survived more than half an hour without being sick. The floor was soon awash with vomit." Howard himself was one of the worst affected, and not surprisingly rehearsed his men relentlessly in exit drill on landing. "Until you're out of there," he barked, "You're rats in a trap."

During 1942 and 1943 British woodworkers were being brought into the business of making gliders, which were mostly put together of plywood and glue, and have been described as 'the most wooden aircraft ever built' – even the controls were of wood: the trick was to make them 'disposable' – as we would say today – while preserving their human contents. The preferred model, which began delivery in the summer of 1943, was the Horsa, followed by the Horsa Mk 2, capable of carrying a pilot and co-pilot and 28 men in battle order, or a quarter-ton truck, or a howitzer.

As the months of 1943 went by, the men of the 52nd gliderborne companies became increasingly frustrated, and all their commanders – but especially John Howard – continued to devise exercises, sports events, and forced marches to occupy their time. Howard even took his men on street-fighting practices, working with live ammunition, in bombed-out areas of Southampton,

Portsmouth and London. All of them were aware that the War Office would not be putting so much energy into the Brigade's training unless some special mission was being planned for them. It had to be connected with the approaching invasion, they guessed, and it might well involve landing behind enemy lines.

They were right.

1944

February 26: Major-General 'Boy' Browning visits Regiment, lectures officers and senior NCOs on 'Invasion Set-Up.'

March 8: Montgomery inspects Division.

March 23: John Howard briefed on a full-scale divisional exercise. 'D' Company to land in gliders near three small bridges in Lechlade and capture them intact.

March 25: To Lechlade for 3-day Exercise BIZZ. D Company dropped in area by truck (no glider landing space available), to capture bridges from 'enemy', and hold until relieved by battalion under Colonel Roberts. General 'Windy' Gale observing.

March 28: Home Leave for Regiment

April 8: Leave cancelled.

April 15: Morning. De-briefing from Exercise BIZZ. Howard and D Company praised for verve in taking bridges and tenacity in holding them.

April 15: Afternoon. Colonel Roberts calls for Major Howard - tells him his Company has been chosen to capture two bridges at start of invasion.

Roberts: "You realise, John, that your Company
will be the spearhead of the invasion. It is a
great honour for the Regiment to be selected to
find troops for this highly important job. But I
feel absolutely confident that you will be able to
pull it off."

Howard: "Yes sir. You can have every confidence in
me and my men."

Roberts: "And John: you realize that this
information is Top Secret."

Howard: "Yes sir."

April 18: Exercise MUSH in Gloucestershire
against a Polish 'enemy.' D Company to attack and
capture two bridges. Mission successful.

May 2: Howard put on X list and given outline of
British plan for invasion of Europe. Invasion to
land not at the Pas-de-Calais as expected by the
Germans, but on the beaches of Normandy.

6th Airborne's task: to protect left or eastern
flank of the Allied bridgehead in Normandy.

Howard's written instructions:

"To seize intact bridges over Caen Canal at
Bénouville and River Orne at Ranville. Hold until
relieved by 7th Parachute Battalion."

Current bridges' defence: garrison of 50 German
troops. 1 German battalion in area, with tanks. 1
Panzer division in Caen.

Bridges wired for demolition, surprise therefore
essential. Noise of aircraft dropping paratroops
would reveal attack, and bridges would be blown

before troops could muster. Therefore gliders
to be used. Six gliders to land as close as
possible to bridges, each carrying platoon
of men to capture bridges and five sappers to
dismantle demolition charges. Howard shown aerial
photographs and detailed model of target area,
and instructed to prepare plan.

May 5: Howard presents his plan to Col. Roberts.
Three platoons are assigned to each bridge:
Canal bridge platoons under Major Howard, River
Bridge platoons under 2 i/c Brian Priday. Plan
takes into account that any glider may land first
and nearest either target. All platoons must
therefore be prepared to initiate any of the
phases of the operation. To avoid friendly fire
in the dark, each platoon to run across bridges
shouting the letter of their platoon - ABCDEF:
Able, Baker, Charlie, Dog, Easy, Fox. (By chance,
Denis Fox's is 'F' platoon.) Roberts reviews
plan. "Sound as a bell," says Roberts.

Training continues.

May 18: All 186 assault troops, infantry and
engineers, assembled for first time for training
together.

May 19: King and Queen, accompanied by Princess
Elizabeth, visits Division.

May 21: Move to Devon to practise on two bridges
similar to French targets. Each platoon to
take turns with each task. Brigadier Nigel
Poett, Commander 5th Para Brigade, and Brigadier
Kindersley, Airlanding Brigade Commander, turn up
to watch.

May 24: Invasion of City of Exeter for a last

night of carousing before return to barracks. Police involved — no charges laid.

May 26: D Company leaves for sealed transit camp at Tarrant Rushton, Dorset. Surrounded by barbed wire. Unable to leave until D-Day.

May 27: Howard given permission to brief his platoon commanders and show them model of the bridge area.

May 28: All ranks shown the model.

May 29: Glider Pilots arrive.

June 1: All men briefed on details of operation. Address by Colonel Roberts, the 52nd's Battalion Commander.

June 3: Men raring to go. Address by Brigadier Kindersley. Cheered by the troops.

June 4: Codeword CROMWELL received: THE INVASION IS ON FOR TONIGHT. D Company makes ready. But weather deteriorates through the day. Heavy rain and gales.

Afternoon: Word arrives: ENTIRE INVASION CANCELLED DUE TO WEATHER CONDITIONS.

So now it is the night of the 4th of June, 1944. One hundred and thirty thousand troops, carried in or supported by 9 battleships, 23 cruisers, 104 destroyers, and 71 large landing craft of various descriptions as well as troop transports, mine sweepers, and merchantmen, in all, nearly 7,000 ships of every type, are poised to cross the narrow ocean, the largest invasion force mankind has ever seen. They are supported by a fleet of 12,000 aircraft. But the ocean tonight is altogether too perilous. The gales continue with a heavy five-foot swell in the Channel. The supreme commander, General Eisenhower, and his staff agonise, afraid to lose the element of surprise, but afraid to compromise the invasion by launching it in fearful weather. The men of D Company watch a film, or down a few beers, or try to rest. The young platoon commanders – it is on record! – sink a bottle of whisky between them. Major John Howard sleeps not at all.

The world waits. And here, and now, let us wait too. For this is the moment when you will find us stepping out of history and into the world of the epic: the epic story of Pegasus Bridge...

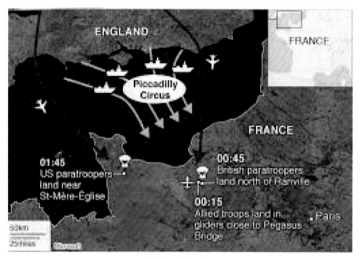

D-Day - the plan

THE EPIC STORY OF
THE CAPTURE OF PEGASUS
AND HORSA BRIDGES

PROLOGUE

It's hard to begin a story like this,
And I reckon to ask the Muses for help
The way poets used to and maybe do still.
After all, this is an epic adventure
In the old style: a handful of men
Especially picked and trained to the hilt
For one great mission: to be the very tip
Of the head of the spear of a great invasion –
The greatest mankind has ever known.
So, Muses wherever you are, come to my aid.
Help me do justice to all, and forget
No one. Help me to paint a true picture.
Help me to see that the brave deeds
Of a few are remembered long years ahead.

[*Reveille sounds*]

1

– Time to be done with the Muses. That call
Has woken the men of the old 52nd
Time out of memory, woken to duty
In the dust of India or the mud of Flanders,
Or the bleak parade grounds around this island.
But for one hundred and eighty picked men
No need for a bugle call today.
They are snatching a few hours of sleep here and there
As the day goes by, between looking out
At the rain and up to the heavy sky,
And checking their kit for the hundredth time.
On the windsocked airfield six gliders sit lifelessly
(Named after Horsa, old Jutish warrior)
Dark in the field, awaiting their pilots,
Awaiting their load, their Halifax tugplanes
Parked close beside them, waiting, waiting.
No one yet sure if tomorrow's the day
– Already postponed after anxious counsel
By a supremely anxious Supreme Commander.
How long can you keep secret the movements
Of hundreds of thousands of men, ships, planes?
But how risk crossing a narrow ocean
In perilous seas whipped up by the wind
And rain, and clouds obscuring the flight
Of the bombers and fighters above? Not long.
The blustery day drives on toward dark:
Sleep nestles fitfully over the land:
The best laid plans hang high in the balance.

2

June the Fifth dawns and it's blustery still;
But then towards noon the winds relent,
And word flashes round the grey coasts of England
That CROMWELL is on for the coming night.
The invasion is on! At last, the invasion!
All is a-bustle at Tarrant Rushton
Sealed camp, home of Letter D Company,
Oxford and Bucks, 52nd of Foot.
The command goes out, brisk and sharp:
"Load the gliders!" And load they do,
Each platoon commander packing their own –
Sweeney, Fox, Brotheridge, Wood, Hooper, Smith –
Under the watchful eye of the Major,
Major John Howard, leader of men,
And of bold Brian Priday, second in command.
What do they take? They take boats and explosives,
Inflatable rafts, Bangalore torpedoes,
"You never know, you might have to blow
Your way through the wire." A soldier remembers:
"Mills grenades (two), number seventy-seven
Phosph'rus smoke (two), ration pack, cooker,
And flotation belts (one), in case you come down
In the drink." David Wood takes a bucket
Of extra grenades in his lap, clearly trusting
That tracer won't find them there on the way over.
Every soldier takes extras – until there's a crisis:
Say the brave glider pilots: "enough is enough -
We'll never get off from the ground overloaded."
Till at last John Howard, leader of men,

Decrees that two men must be dropped from each glider,
And those left behind stand there unbelieving,
Tears in their eyes to be missing the show.

All drift to the NAAFI for one last meal,
All spoiled with treats. Each is given a pack,
With Benzedrine tablets and money – French money
In case they get lost; and silk maps of Europe,
A miniature compass sewn on to the fly
Of their trousers and files sewn into their pockets
To saw their way out of a prison if taken.
They blacken their faces for night operations.
Three years they have trained, and this is the night:
It is real, you touch it and taste it. We're here
Because we are here, because we are here.

Visitors call from Headquarters: first Monty,
To view the six gliders and talk to the pilots.
"Bring back as many of the chaps as you can,"
He says to John Howard. John Howard: "Yes, sir."
Now General Gale, 'Windy' Gale as they call him,
Who speaks to the men of the coming invasion.
Colonel Mike Roberts and Adjutant Tillett
Visit again to keep up the spirits
 Of men they've been training and known for so long,
And wish them the best till they meet up in France.

3

Twenty-two hundred hours: lorries arrive,
To carry them, decked out like Christmas trees,
To the planes. The NAAFI girls weep as they wave
Farewell. At the field an air force chap
Comes round to the men with a dixie of tea.
They fill their mugs. "Mm, good – 'arf a mo'! –
There's rum in it, mates!" They swallow it down.
Twenty-two thirty and out to the gliders.
Twenty-three to a plane plus five sappers and pilots:
Sappers of course to dismantle explosives
and save both the bridges intact if they can.
Twelve to each side they strap themselves in.
Last up the platoon sergeants through the rear door
And in front the platoon commanders and pilots.

Twenty-two fifty, and Major John Howard
Visits each glider and thanks all his men
For their help and their spirits throughout the long years.
He leaves and the doors are slammed shut. And they wait.
And they wait. And they wait. In silence they wait.
Twenty-two-fifty-eight and – Listen! The roar
Of John Howard's glider being towed down the runway,
Den Brotheridge and his men crammed into the hull.

Twenty-two-fifty-nine and it sails up the air
And into the dark of the storm-ridden sky:
To be chased at eleven by glider the second,
Then third, then fourth, then fifth, then sixth,

Each a minute apart on the wings of the night.
"A suicide mission," staff officers called it,
"A Military Cross if you come out alive!
To land six lumbering gliders in darkness
Right next to two bridges each bristling with Germans,
And capture them under the enemy's nose?
Why it's crazy!" Well, crazy or not, here they are.

4

Over the soft combes of England they fly
Over the darkened towns and villages,
Over the ancient New Forest and over
The gentle South Downs, turning southward at Bognor,
To cross the sea-coast and head toward France.
Below them, flexing its muscles in darkness,
A mighty host – British, Canadian, American –
Feel engines stirring beneath their feet
In ships of the line from Cornwall to Kent:
Battleships, minesweepers, cruisers, destroyers,
Landing-craft, motor torpedo boats, merchantmen,
– Soldiers and sailors poised for invasion,
Nose out of port to the open sea.
And above our six gliders, to cover their crossing,
Droning in chorus fly bombers in hundreds,
In tight formation, loaded with death,
For targets throughout Hitler's stolen domains.
Our gliders fly on, tugged southward to France
By Halifax bombers at six thousand feet.

5

Who would imagine the mission before them?
Inside the hull of one glider is silence,
The glow of a few cigarettes in the dark:
In others they're singing "Roll out the Barrel!",
Or "I'm forever blowing bubbles", or joking,
Or quietly coping with fear and airsickness.
And up in the cockpits the pilots are straining
– Wallwork, Boland, Barkway and Pearson,
Lawrence and Howard, staff sergeants all –
Straining to hold their tugplanes in view
And preparing the moment to cast off the towlines,
And mentally gearing to land on a sixpence,
And knowing the whole operation depends
On skill, courage and luck; and all those men
Sitting behind them and trusting their judgement.
Fair stands the wind for France, and fair
The midnight sky, moon coming and going,
Below them that perilous, narrow ocean,
Crossed and re-crossed over the centuries.

Now subaltern Sweeney can see up ahead
Through the perspex the long, long line of spray
Where the sea meets the moon-blanched land.
France! The dull crump of enemy fire,
And the beams of searchlights criss-crossing the sky.
This is the moment. "Casting off!"
Shout the pilots, and pulling a wood-crafted lever
Unhitch their gliders. The bombers roar off
On a new and deadly mission of their own.

And suddenly the gliders are alone and soundless –
Night air whispering over their wings –
And the men fall silent. There's no going back -
Pilots and co-pilots watching and calling out
Air speed, direction, and minutes to fly.
Six thousand feet, five thousand, four thousand, three:
A sharp turn at three minutes, another at two,
Then fifteen hundred and doors are slid open,
Below them the vasty fields of France:
"God Almighty! I can see trees!" One remembers –
And the sweet damp scent of the Normandy soil;
And, cutting two shining paths through the grassland,
There, the River Orne and the Caen Canal,
Shining like silver in light of the moon:
Below them the bridges, sharp in that moonlight,
Uncannily aping the models they've studied.
The pilots are signalling: "Time to prepare!"
In each glider the soldiers, so many times practised,
Their rifles all pointing straight downward for safety,
Link arms and pull up their feet from the deck.
The gliders lurch queasily as they descend,
The pilots directing them best as they can.
Three platoons to each bridge: that is the plan.
John Howard with Den Brotheridge, David Wood, Sandy Smith,
And their men to land by the canal's swing bridge,
And Priday with Hooper and Sweeney and Fox
To drop a few hundred yards beyond
At the other and longer bridge over the river.
Intelligence warned them the fields they're to land in

May be peppered with poles to obstruct such a landing –
Devices referred to as Rommel's Asparagus.
No way to avoid them, they watch and they pray.

First Pilot Wallwork with Howard and Brotheridge
Speeds down through the darkness, the men clutching tight.
Closer. And closer. Then: crash! To the ground –
Sparks shooting, wood splintering, wheels shearing clean,
Safety straps snapping, the soldiers go flying,
The racket infernal, yes, hell is let loose,
As they screech on their belly through Normandy loam,
Over the field bumping and grinding.
Then finally still. Jim Wallwork has made it!
A miracle landing just yards from the bridge.
For a second they stare, all catching their balance.
They listen for stuttering enemy fire.
Not a sound. The night echoes back their silence.
Now spring into action: Den Brotheridge first
Smashes out through the door, his soldiers come stumbling
After him, falling on grass with their burdens
Of rifles, grenades, ammunition and packs.
Others come tumbling out from the rear,
All of them taking defensive positions
In arrow formation encircling the wreck.
Still no response from an enemy sleeping -
Surprise is the weapon still warm in their hands:
Not a moment to waste. "Follow me!" whispers Brotheridge
And forms up a section of men to attack.
Just as they start out, from the inner defences
A machine-gun opens its rat-a-tat fire.

A phosphorus smoke bomb gives cover to Bailey
To race to the pillbox this side of the bridge
And drop a whole pile of grenades through the slits.
By now the first section, furiously shooting
With Brens, Stens and rifles, straight from the hip,
Den Brotheridge shouting out 'Dog! Dog! Dog!'
Storms through the wire and on to the bridge.

6

Meantime Glider Two smashes down through the night,
Hitting the ground with a shattering thump,
Bouncing just once before crashing again,
And splitting apart with the shock of the impact,
But thanks to the brilliance of Oliver Boland
Landing miraculously close to the first;
David Wood tossed out of the plane but unhurt,
His store of grenades still clutched in his arms,
His lads safe too though shaken and bruised.
And there is John Howard, leader of men,
Greeting them by the perimeter wire,
With a "Good show, chaps – get on with it now!"
"Forward!" says young David Wood in a whisper,
Knowing his job is to go for the trenches
This side of the bridge and to clear out the enemy.
He gathers his men and goes off at the double.

And now the third glider is arrowing down
Overloaded and heading directly on target –
Too sharply, too fast, too directly on target,
For there in the moonlight, crumpled and broken,

Lies David Wood's glider smack in its path.
But at the last moment, Geoff Barkway, brave pilot,
Wrenches his glider wheels out of the way,
Breaking its frail wooden fabric in half
To come to a juddering stop in a pond,
Propelling himself right clean through the perspex
With subaltern Sandy Smith shot out alongside.
In his violent fall Sandy's knee has been wrenched
But he pulls himself out of the mud and assembles
His men to advance on the bridge, now scene
Of a fierce gunfight with the woken defenders.

7

Soon, soon the canal bridge is captured and won,
But alas! Denham Brotheridge racing across
Has been caught in the fire of a Spandau machine gun;
Shot in the neck he falls on the bridge,
And not an hour later this handsomest man,
Beloved of his men, fellow-officers too,
Only two weeks away from becoming a father,
Has given his life for the cause of freedom,
First of the thousands to die that day,
That longest day of the Great Invasion.
Major John Howard, leader of men,
Is heartstruck to hear the loss of his friend,
But no time to grieve: the mop-up continues.
David Wood has been clearing his trenches of Germans,
But he and his sergeant are caught in a burst
From a Schmeisser machine pistol, deadliest of weapons,
And David is felled to the ground, his leg shattered –

Sergeant Leather beside him, both out of action.
And young Corporal Godbold assumes their command.
Meantime the sappers are under the bridge
Rend'ring it safe from a timed demolition.
They find that the bridge has been heavily wired,
But charges had not been laid to explode it.

Sandy Smith leads his men over the bridge
To strengthen the soldiers of Brotheridge's platoon
(Now commanded by valiant Corporal Bailey),
And winkle out fast the remaining defenders
Alongside the road that leads on to Bénouville.
But within a few seconds – or minutes: who knows
In a battle? – a stick grenade thrown from a trench
Strikes Sandy a blow on the wrist and explodes,
Smashing the bones and blasting the flesh:
'No more cricket,' thinks Sandy, a consummate player,
but picks himself up and goes on into action.

8

And what of the river bridge, paces away?
Where are Priday, and Hooper, and Sweeney, and Fox?
Brian Priday's glider is not to be seen,
And Major John Howard is fearing the worst.
It was to be quite twenty-four hours on –
Having been landed ten miles from their target –
That Priday and Hooper returned to D Company,
Fighting their way through pockets of enemy,
And losing a number of men on the journey.

Subaltern Fox has his usual luck –
Landing exactly as planned by the river,
Waiting a second for rattle of gunfire,
Imagining soon to be riddled with bullets.
But once again, total surprise, and in silence
He gathers his men and makes fast for the river bridge,
Crossing it crying out "Fox! Fox! Fox!"
And ready to mow down any defenders.
Two men run away, scared off by a mortar.
No one else. The bridge is deserted. They halt
And start to prepare for a counter-attack,
While sappers crawl under to check for explosives.

9

Meantime Sweeney's glider has not been so lucky.
As it comes to the landing zone, Pearson the pilot
Cries out in alarm "we're dropping too fast!"
They hit the deck four hundred yards from the bridge,
Grinding on stony soil over the field
And coming to rest with a smash and a crash.
Out they all leap and gather defensively,
Then start out hot foot to the bridge in the distance,
But in a few yards they are up to the waist
In a duckpond, from which in a certain disorder
They scramble to free themselves. As they emerge,
They hear sounds of firing from down the canal.
Not a second to waste. They make for their target,
And reaching the bridge they pound straight across it,
Crying "Baker! Baker!" and secretly thinking:
"Any moment it might blow up under our feet!"

But it holds firm and still as they canter across:
Triumphantly Sweeney and all his men
Have done the impossible: captured their bridge!
But then on the eastern approach they see figures,
Shadowy figures they think may be Germans,
Till from the shadows emerges an officer,
Calmly inhaling a fresh cigarette.
It is Subaltern Fox. "What is happening, Fox?"
Pants Sweeney, still dripping with water and mud.
"Oh, the exercise went very well," says Fox,
"But how can we tell who's alive and who's not?
 I'm damned if I can find any umpires." –
A comment for which Fox has always been famous.
A signal is sent to John Howard's command post:
"River bridge captured!" And Corporal Tappenden
Sends out the codewords so keenly awaited
By those who have planned the whole mighty invasion:
"Ham and Jam! Ham and Jam! Ham and Jam! Ham and Jam!"
("Both bridges – intact – are now in our hands!")
Ted Tappenden waits for his call to be answered:
"Ham and Jam! Ham and Jam! Ham and Jam! Ham and Jam!"
But radio contact is lost for a while
And no one is there to acknowledge his message…
"Ham and Jam! Ham and Jam! Ham and Jam! Ham and Jam!"
Ted finds himself getting all hoarse and frustrated:
"Ham and Jam! Ham and Jam! Ham – and bloody Jam!"
Till finally hearing a crackling acknowledgment:
"Message received and understood."

10

Meantime Major Howard, leader of men,
Picks up his whistle and pipes out the signal:
Di-di-di-dah! Di-di-di-dah! Di-di-di-dah! Di-di-di-dah!
V, V, V for Victory!
For while his brave gliders accomplish their mission,
East of the bridges 5th Para Brigade
Have been dropping in parachutes over the land:
First mission: to capture the bridges if Howard
And Letter 'D' Company fail in their task.
Their landings dispersed much wider than planned,
They are cheered by the Victory sign on the whistle
And guided across in the dark to their target.
Once there, in numbers sadly reduced
From the six hundred men that were planned to be massing,
They man the two bridges' outer defences.
So at zero three thirty John Howard's platoons
Are well reinforced: their duty near done.

11

In battle it's helpful and even commanded
To think of the enemy only as obstacles.
Hard to forget that first bayonet practice,
Ten boys in men's uniform lined up in rows,
Their rifles held fast at the ready, arm straight,
Each bayonet fixed, steel wicked and gleaming,
And there down the field, in a parallel row,
Ten sacks hanging helplessly, bulging with straw.
Some hard-bitten sergeant barks out the order:
"Charge!" And the boys go galloping forward,

To close with the enemy, knifing their victims
With tentative, timid, reluctant thrusts.
"Pathetic," yells Sergeant Hardbitten: "Get back 'ere,
Yer bunch o' wet schoolgirls. This time when I give
The command, let me 'ear you: yell at the top of your
Nancified lungs, and kill, kill, kill!
Wait for it now… Get ready and – charge!"
And slowly reluctance gives over to madness:
Screaming like furies unjointing their prey
They stab and they twist and they slice and they slash.
"That's better," cries Sergeant Hardbitten, his boys
Fair pleased with themselves, and the praise they have won.
So the young soldier-boy conquers his kindliness,
Working to pattern his fear into anger,
Soon to seem cool in the face of destruction,
Knowing the enemy back in *his* homeland
Has worked the same magic to harden his heart.
"Töte, töte, töte, töte!"
Yells the hardbitten Unteroffizier,
As the young German boys, dressed in men's uniform,
Stab, and twist, and slice, and slash.
So the world goes, so the world goes.

12

So what of those plucky defenders? How plucky?
Caught with their trousers down, never expecting
Attack, not tonight, in the still rough weather,
And far, far away from the beaches of Calais
Where all Hitler's generals expect the invasion.
The soldiers manning the western defences

Are most of them shipped from the eastern front
Too old or uncertain to grapple with Russians,
And some are young conscripts from Nazified nations
Or joined Hitler's armies for food and a bed.
On the canal bridge two guards are on duty,
Who give the alarm, and engage the attackers.
But guards on the river bridge, as we have seen,
Scamper away. Denis Fox and his men,
Told to leave Sweeney on guard at the river
And move to assist along the canal
By clearing the trenches surrounding the bridge,
Discover a posse of soldiers asleep
In an underground dugout, who, shaken awake
By a bunch of mysterious clowns with black faces,
Think their mates are playing a practical joke,
And tell them to scarper and turn back to sleep:
Not quite the response of a fearsome foe.

Meanwhile their great leader, Herr Commandant,
Is having a night of it down in the town,
When he hears of the raid, and calls for his driver
And motorbike escort to hurry him back.
He grinds right along in his open half-track,
Where Sweeney's brave men are lying in wait.
They shoot at the escort who swerves to the ground,
But the officer speeds through the hail of fire
And on to the bridge, where a lobbed grenade
Explodes in the vehicle, stopped in its tracks,
Killing driver and wounding our Herr Commandant.
As they're treating his wounds, the fanatical Nazi

Unleashes a flood of abuse on his captors:
"You're going to be thrown back into the sea!
Mein Führer will conquer you: he will prevail!"

13

And now from the bridges Major John Howard
Sends Fox and his lads on into Bénouville,
And as they move cautiously into the town
They hear the approach of what sounds like a tank:
Sergeant Thornton deploys his anti-tank weapon,
As up the road from the sea, not one,
Not two, not three, but four come grinding
As fast as they can to protect the bridges.
Shaking, he says, like a leaf he waits
For the leader to come within range – and then Boom!
He hits the vehicle plum in the middle.
It explodes like a thousand fireworks, men
Jumping out of it running for cover, the driver
Lying there horribly wounded and screaming,
Until Private Clare can stand it no longer:
He runs to the German and picks him up bodily
Taking him back to the first aid post.
What can you do for a man like that,
Both of his feet blown off in the blast?
Morphine of course; he will die before morning.
So the world goes, so the world goes.

The flaming vehicle lights up the sky,
Blocking the road for the armour behind it,
And forcing them all to withdraw until daylight -

But serving as beacon for paratroops dropping
East of the bridges to find their way there.
Slowly the holding force builds its strength
And prepares for sharp-shooting from enemy snipers
And for ferocious counter-attacks.

14

And where is the famous Panzer Division
Of tanks in reserve in the city of Caen?
Why has it not burst out of its barracks
And stormed to the bridges to smash the attackers?
Only much later the story is told
By its bitter commander, Hans von Luck,
That a Panzer Division could not be deployed
Without the express consent of "Mein Führer":
Hitler, snoring away in Berlin,
Not a single soul daring to shake him awake.
So maniacal folly will finally doom itself
Drowned in the shit of its own making.
For while the Panzer Divisions stand idle
Throughout the length of the western defences,
The whole vast host of the Allied invasion
Has sailed through the darkness. A curtain of gunfire
Rains on the dawning coasts of France,
And now the first landings on Juno, on Gold,
On Sword and on Utah and Omaha beaches
Complete the mightiest crossing in history
Over that perilous narrow ocean:
As American, British, Canadian divisions
Sail to the rescue of the world.

15

As dawn begins to break far in the east,
The little cafe beside the canal bridge,
Shuttered against the battle outside,
Its terrified owners fled down to the cellar,
Now hears that the language around it is English,
And opens its doors and its hearts to the raiders:
The Gondrées, Georges and Thérèse, now embrace them,
And Georges goes out with a spade to the garden
To dig up a hundred bottles of bubbly,
Hidden so long from the thirsty Germans,
To celebrate this unbelievable happening:
O joie! La libération de la France!

16

And with the dawn light, as Brigadier Poett
And his paras secure their positions around
The canal and the river bridge, holding them safe,
Major John Howard, leader of men,
Grimly reflects on his casualty list:
One officer dead, two seriously wounded;
A whole glider missing and yet to resurface;
Lance-Corporal Greenhalgh drowned on the landing;
And, wounded in action, twelve other ranks.
A sad enough tally; but taken in all
A miraculous toll for a suicide mission
Where many thought no one would come out alive.
"Capture the bridges and hold till relieved":
That was the order. The order's obeyed.

The pluck of a handful of valiant men
Has set into motion the hugest of battles,
Where thousands and thousands of people will perish
In the next bitter months; but one year on
The sunshine of peace will spread over the land.
 Hitler will shoot himself out of the world:
"Mein Führer" is dead. He has NOT prevailed.

AFTERMATH

So ends one telling of the story of the capture of the canal and river bridges, renamed 'Pegasus' and – much later – 'Horsa' by the French government. Is my story definitive? Of course not – there is so much more. First, we must be clear: this was, I believe, the first operation of D-Day, carried out on the continent of Europe, by a concerted body of Allied troops.

But it was not the first blow struck for the liberation of Europe. Let us not forget the courageous work of the French Resistance in the days leading up to the invasion. On the night before

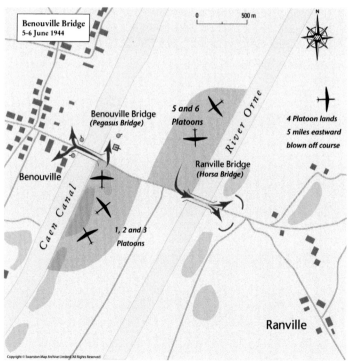

Benouville Bridge
5-6 June 1944

0   500 m

N

Benouville Bridge
(Pegasus Bridge)

5 and 6
Platoons

River Orne

4 Platoon lands
5 miles eastward
blown off course

Benouville

Ranville Bridge
(Horsa Bridge)

Caen Canal

1, 2 and 3
Platoons

Ranville

Copyright © Swanston Map Archive Limited. All Rights Reserved

D Day, after a coded message was sent out on the BBC, over a thousand incidents took place, destroying communication systems, blowing up roads and railways all along the Channel coast. Let us remember among these brave folk the Gondrées, owners of the little café beside the canal. Thérèse, brought up in Alsace-Lorraine, understood German, and kept her ears open for any nuggets let drop in her café by the German garrison guarding the bridges. She passed these to Georges, who bicycled into Caen and shared them with the local Resistance. Within 24 hours the information was in London. It was partly owing to the Gondrées that John Howard and his men had such precise knowledge of the bridge defences before they landed.

Nor, we think, were these men of the 52nd the first to land in France. We must also pay tribute to the 'pathfinders', the brave English, American and Canadian paratroopers who dropped alone around the same time into the Landing Zones to provide beacons for their comrades landing en masse a little later. The first Allied soldier to alight on French soil that momentous night is in fact believed to have been Lieutenant Poole of the 5th Para Brigade. We must remember all the men of 6th Airborne Division, proudly wearing their Pegasus flash, including the rest of the 52nd, who suffered grievous losses securing the eastern approaches to the Invasion beaches, and especially in taking the battery on the coast at Merville.

We must also pay tribute to all the people working behind the scenes to make the mission possible. The planners of the whole D-Day operation; the brave co-pilots of the gliders, and the pilots of the tug-planes which towed them to the French coast; the engineers, under the command of Captain Jock Nielson and Lieutenant Bence, who accompanied the mission, cleared the bridges and then joined in their defence; the designers and builders of the Horsa gliders which carried the Pegasus Bridge attackers… and the list goes on.

Nor does our telling pay proper tribute to the families – wives, parents, grandparents, brothers and sisters, children, uncles and aunts, fiancées, partners – of all those men who took part in the Pegasus Bridge show. Their love and support, as with all wars, helped sustain the courage and spirits of those men of the 52nd.

There was one episode which took place later that day which is a little outside the scope of our story. In the early afternoon, while they were taking a quick nap, Tod Sweeney turned to Denis Fox and said, "Denis, I can hear bagpipes!" "Don't be crazy, Tod. We're in the middle of France!" But Tod was right. They looked down the road from Ouistreham and the sea, and there, striding along in the sunshine at the head of the Lovat Scouts was Lord Lovat himself, and beside him Piper Millins, playing "Blue Bonnets Over The Border" for all he was worth. Behind them marched the Commandos of the First Special Service Brigade. They were the first troops from the beach landings that Howard's men had seen, and this was the first link-up of seaborne and airborne forces. According to one account, everybody threw their rifles on the ground, kissing and hugging each other – men with tears rolling down their cheeks. Such is the power of music – even, or perhaps especially, the music of the pipes. "Sorry, two and a half minutes late," said Lord Lovat airily to Brigadier Poett, as he crossed the bridge and turned back north along the canal. Sadly, many of the commandos behind him were picked off by snipers as they crossed the bridges behind Lovat and his piper.

What is the verdict of history on the Pegasus Bridge affair? A few days after the raid, a party of senior Russian officers was sent by Stalin to gauge progress on the Western Front, for which he had been calling for so many months and years. They were proudly taken to the bridges, shown the gliders and given an account of the attack. Their reaction was unexpected. Apparently, they were not at all impressed. Why? Because they absolutely refused to believe it. They were convinced that the gliders could not possibly have landed on such a tiny field, and that they must have been towed there later and arranged to 'look like a good show'.

The landing was indeed miraculous. Air-Chief-Marshall Leigh-Mallory described it as "the greatest feat of flying of World War Two."

About the operation as a whole, the American military historian Stephen Ambrose has this to say:

"At a minimum, failure at Pegasus Bridge would have made D-Day much more costly to the Allies, and especially to the 6th Airborne Division. At a maximum, failure at Pegasus Bridge might have meant failure for the invasion as a whole, with consequences for world history too staggering to contemplate."

Let us leave this saga of modern heroes, not beside the bridges they captured with such courage and held with such tenacity, but among those of them who did not survive to appreciate the full glory of what was achieved. On the night following their first triumphant operation, for which they had trained for three years, Letter D company had rejoined the rest of the 52nd in the village of Ranville, and next day became bogged down in a ferocious struggle in the nearby hamlet of Escoville. By mid-afternoon, half the Company had become casualties. In September, after ninety-one days of continuous battle, D Company was withdrawn to England. Howard was the only officer still on his feet. All the sergeants and most of the corporals were gone. All told, D Company had fallen from its D-Day strength of 181 men to 40.

Most of the men of the 52nd who fell in Normandy are buried in Ranville cemetery, close to the bridges. But it's worth recalling the Latin inscription above another cemetery in Bayeux, commemorating the nearly 2000 men who died in Normandy and have no known grave:

NOS A GULIELMO VICTI VICTORIS PATRIAM LIBERAVIMUS

WE, ONCE CONQUERED BY WILLIAM, HAVE NOW SET FREE THE CONQUEROR'S NATIVE LAND

So the wheel comes full circle: that perilous narrow ocean has brought conquerors both ways.

EPILOGUE

Years have gone by since that longest day.
But picture one golden afternoon –
With June again in her flaming glory,
The sun riding high over corn and clover –
When Colonel Tod Sweeney, now old and infirm,
Meets up with Herr Oberst Hans von Luck,
At Pegasus Bridge beside the canal.
And after a long and convivial lunch,
The two distinguished military gentlemen
Hobble along the road to Ranville.
"When we come to the cemet'ry gate," says Tod,
"We pause for a moment, almost embarrassed.
Then each turn away, each to the place
Where our fallen comrades are lying forever:
Each to remember, each to mourn.
And as we recall those beautiful dead,
At opposite ends of the burial ground,
I wonder again at the meaning of war,
The pity of war, the folly of war,
The waste, the crime, the needlessness."
Two old men in a burial ground,
Weeping together, but weeping apart,
As the sun rides down, rides down, rides down,
Down to the perilous narrow ocean,
As the sun rides down to the western sea.

Illustration Credits

Cover illustration based on the original oil painting 'Operation Deadstick' by Michael Turner.

The English Channel. Courtesy of Wikimedia.

P. 1   The Death of King Harold. Battle of Hastings, 1066. Detail of the Bayeux Tapestry - 11th Century. © with special permission from the City of Bayeux.

P. 3   Henry V before Harfleur. Illuminated manuscript, 15th Century.

P. 5   Napoleon and John Bull: 'Conversation across the Water'. Satirical cartoon, 1803-4.

P. 6   View of Trenches World War One. © courtesy of Everett Collection/Shutterstock.com.

P. 9   Adolf Hitler, late 1930s, courtesy of Everett Collection/Shutterstock.com

P. 11   The Retreat from Dunkirk. Painting by Charles Ernest Cundall. Image © courtesy of Imperial War Museum.

P. 15   Photo of John Howard. Image courtesy of Penny Bates (daughter of John Howard).

P. 17   Platoon of Men in Horsa Glider. Image © courtesy of Imperial War Museum.

P. 24   Tarrant Rushton Airfield 1944. Image © courtesy of Imperial War Museum.

P. 25   Map of Invasion, D-Day 1944. Image © courtesy of Pegasus Bridge Museum.

P. 47   Map of Pegasus and Horsa Bridges. ©courtesy of The Map Archive.

P. 50   Gliders after landing at Pegasus Bridge. June 1944. Image © courtesy of Imperial War Museum.

P. 53   Ranville War Cemetery at Sunset. Image © courtesy of Alamy